Fl0ating and
Sinking

Karen Bryant-Mole

Heinemann
Interactive Library
Des Plaines, Illinois

First published in the United States by Heinemann Interactive Library,
an imprint of Reed Educational & Professional Publishing,
1350 East Touhy Avenue, Suite 240 West
Des Plaines, IL 60018

Printed in Hong Kong / China
Designed by Jean Wheeler
Commissioned photography by Zul Mukhida
Consultant—Hazel Grice

© BryantMole Books 1998

02 01 00 99 98
10 9 8 7 6 5 4 3 2 1

Library of Congress Cataloging-in-Publication Data
Bryant-Mole, Karen.
    Floating and sinking / by Karen Bryant-Mole.
      p.   cm. -- (Science all around me)
    Includes bibliographical references and index.
    Summary: Describes why things float or sink and presents simple
experiments to demonstrate the scientific principles involved.
    ISBN 1-57572-627-0 (library binding)
    1. Floating bodies--Juvenile literature. 2. Floating bodies-
-Experiments--Juvenile literature. [1. Floating bodies-
-Experiments. 2. Archimedes' principle--Experiments. 3. Water-
-Experiments. 4. Experiments.] I. Title. II. Series.
QC147.B79   1998
532'.25--dc21
                                   97-41946
                                       CIP
                                       AC

A number of questions are posed in this book. They are designed
to consolidate children's understanding by encouraging further
exploration of the science in their everyday lives.

Acknowledgements
The Publishers would like to thank the following for permission to reproduce photographs: Eye Ubiquitous P. 4, (S.
Greenland), P. 16 (A. Cudbertson); Positive Images pp. 6, 8, 10, 18, 20; Tony Stone Images p. 14 (David Schultz); Zefa p. 22.

Every effort had been made to contact copyright holders of any material reproduced in this book. Any omissions will
be rectified in subsequent printings if notice is given to the Publisher.

Words that appear in the text in bold can be found in the glossary.

Contents

Floating   4

Sinking   6

Size   8

Heaviness   10

Pushing Water   12

Water Pushes Back   14

Under the Water   16

Materials   18

Air   20

Waterproof   22

More Books to Read   24

Glossary   24

Index   24

Floating

The boy in this boat is moving through water without getting wet. This is because his boat floats.

Anything that stays at the top of water is said to float.

(i) *Small sailing boats are called "dinghies."*

See for yourself...

Brian wanted to find some
things that could float.

He tested many different things
by placing them in
a bowl of water.

He found five things
that could float.

Sinking

When something that cannot float is put into water, it sinks.

This **anchor** can't float. It has sunk to the bottom of the water.

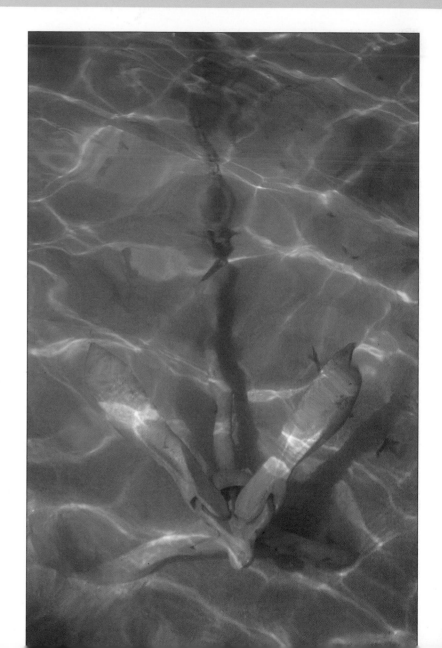

? *What do you think might be on the other end of the chain?*

6

See for yourself...

Melissa is testing some things to see which float and which sink.

She has put them into two groups. Can you guess which group floats and which group sinks?

Brian's test will give you a clue!

7

Size

What makes some things float and some things sink?
Size could be important. But look, this large boat and
this small boat both float.

(i) *A large stone and a small stone would both sink.*

See for yourself...

Jessica has done a test with objects that are about the same size and shape.

She has discovered that some float and some sink.

Size might be important but it can't be the only thing that matters.

Heaviness

Whether or not something can float could have to do with how much it **weighs**.

Heavy things might sink and light things might float.

But look, this log and these leaves both float.

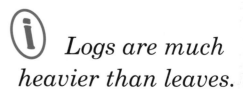 *Logs are much heavier than leaves.*

See for yourself...

Adam is testing some objects that all weigh about the same.

He thought they would all float or all sink. But some float and some sink.

Weight might be important but it can't be the only thing that matters.

Pushing Water

To understand why things float, we need to know what happens when something is put into water.

When the plates were put into this bowl, they pushed the water out of the way to make space for themselves.

This is called "displacement."

Where do you think the displaced water has gone?

See for yourself...

Alex carefully filled two pitchers with water.

She put a large stone into one pitcher. Water was displaced into a cup in front of the pitcher.

When she tried this with a smaller stone, less water was displaced.

13

Water Pushes Back

As these tree trunks roll into the water, they push the water out of the way to make room for themselves.

The water pushes back, trying to get back into the space it was in.

(i) *If the water pushes back strongly enough, an object will float.*

See for yourself...

Jonathan put a ping-pong ball into a glass of water.

He is trying to push it down under the water.

He can feel the water that is being pushed out of the way pushing back.

Under the Water

This boat has been taken out of the water.

You can see that much of the boat is usually under the water. The boat is a big shape for the water to push against.

The more of something there is for water to push against, the more likely it is to float.

See for yourself...

Brian found two pieces of clay that were both the same weight.

He rolled one into a ball. He made the other into a boat shape.

The ball-shaped piece sinks. The boat-shaped piece floats because the clay is spread out into a big shape there is more clay for the water to push against.

Materials

Whether something floats or sinks depends on both its weight and its size.

This sailboard is big but it is very light and so it floats.

Something that is light for its size is more likely to float than something that is heavy for its size.

See for yourself...

Melissa found that the **material** that things are made of is important.

Things made of **solid** wood or Styrofoam seem to float more easily than things made of solid metal or stone.

Air

This huge ship is made of metal.

If it was made of solid metal it would sink. But most of the space inside the ship is full of air.

(i) *Air makes things light for their size and helps them to float.*

See for yourself...

Billy is testing some bath toys.

He has found that many of them are hollow.

Hollow things aren't empty. They are full of air.

21

Waterproof

Some **materials soak up** water.

If something soaks up a lot of water, it may sink.

This boat has special paint on it. It stops the water soaking into the wood underneath.

ⓘ *Materials that do not soak up water are called "waterproof."*

See for yourself...

Alex floated pieces of cardboard, **fabric**, plastic, and foil on water.

She wanted to find out which materials were waterproof.

A few hours later, both the cardboard and the fabric had soaked up water and sunk.

Glossary

anchor a heavy metal object used to keep boats in place

fabric cloth

material what things are made from

soak up suck up

solid the same all the way through, not hollow

weighs how heavy something is

Index

air 20–21
displacement 12, 13
floating 4–5, 7–12, 14, 16–18, 20, 23
heaviness 10–11, 18
hollow 21
lightness 18, 20
materials 19, 22
pushing 12, 14–17
sinking 6–11, 17, 20, 22, 23
size 8–9, 18, 20
waterproof 22–23
weight 10, 11, 17, 18

More Books to Read

Challomer, Jack. *Floating and Sinking*. Chatham, NJ: Raintree Steck-Vaughn. 1996. An older reader can help you with this book.

Ward, Alan. *Water & Floating*. Danbury, CT: Franklin Watts. 1992.